In

My

Opinion

By

Bruce Dolan Smith

Revised June 2016

Published by BDS Distributors

Copyright 2015 by BDS Distributors

This book is dedicated to all of our service personnel which have fought in all of our wars. Either our current war we are in right now or back to WW1. I also would like to mention all branches of our government all the way from our local government to our president. If it was not for anyone of them we as a United States cannot progress to where we need to go.

If you like what I stand for

then vote for me

for Town Council in Phillipsburg

Nov 2017

I ask for you to give me a

chance

If you like what I do for Phillipsburg

then keep me as

Councilman

Introduction

As you read my policatial agenda some of you may disagree with me. You will find that one person may not like one thing that is on my agenda but they will like something else which is on my agenda. Everything that I am for I have experienced in my life time.

Last year (November 2013) I ran for councilman in my town. My friends and I passed out 500 brochures. Out of that I received 260 votes. My campaign ran for only 3 days. This tells me if I was to start my campaigned a lot early I would have received more votes. I am going to run again for councilman in the town that I live in now. I will start my campaigned a lot earlier. As I talk to people now I am already starting my campaign. I tell the people to give me a chance. If they do not like my politics after my term is over then ok I will not run again. However if they do like the job I have done then vote for me again.

My politics is not only for Phillipsburg, NJ but it is for every single town in America.

If you like what I stand for then let you voice be heard. Pass this book on to all your friends and family. You can email me if you want to at my email address below. I will try to get back to you as soon as I can.

Thank you

God Bless

Bruce D. Smith

Table of Contents

Chapter One

911

I can remember to this very day when I was told that our country was under attack. At first I did not believe it however when I saw it on the news then I knew it was for real. When I went home I turned the TV on. President Bush was at a school in Sarasota, Florida. One of the secret service personnel went over to the President and spoke to him quietly. President Bush handled the news very well considering where he was at that time. Immediately after his visit with the school in Sarasota President Bush spoke to the country and told us what we all did not want to hear. He told us many lives have been lost that day. As days went by the worse news we heard was the number of lives lost was climbing. If I remember correctly there were about 3,000 men, women and children killed in this unnecessary act. Even till this day people are dying because of what it did to their health at that time. I think anyone who was in the area of the Word Trade Center and was harmed in any way should be helped. The government should help these people out without question. There are a lot of people suffering and they are not getting help. A lot of them are still unable to work. We as a country need to help them out. Let us not make them suffer any longer. Let us give them the help they need.

President Bush was not in office very long when 911 happened. He had to make decisions I do not think he wanted to do but he was given no choice. He did not want to go to war however Osama bin Laden forced this on him. Thank God today we captured Osama bin Laden and he was put to death immediately.

We will always be faced with the possibility of going to war. Our country is always ready to defend the constitution if we have to. I pray and hope we will never have to go to war again. I pray for Peace not only in our homeland but also overseas.

Hours after the attack people went to churches. There is this small church right in the area of the World Trade Center 100s if not more flooded the church. For months people searched their faith to help sort this nightmare we were living in. If I remember correctly the first two years churches saw a rise in membership or just attending on a regular basis. My question is why then today do we not see the same people in church. We just do not need to go to church when bad things happen we should go more often. This helps strengthens us so we can handle the problems or tribulations we all face on a daily basis. By going to church on a regular basis prepares all of us to help each other in our own time of need. It does not matter what faith or religion you are we all need God to help us on a daily basis. So my suggestions to you if you are not attending your church on a regular basis start now do not wait till the next 911 happens.

St. Paul's Chapel

Chapter Two

Who started the Iraq war?

We all know who started this war.

First off President George Bush Jr. lied to us about Iraq having weapons of mass destruction. He only sent 50 troops to Afghanistan and sent thousands troops to Iraq. Once we got Saddam Hussein and hung him we should have left Iraq and went full force into Afghanistan. If we did so we would not be where we are today.

Here is my view point on the war. It was Osama bin Laden that started all of this. Yes I know there were many unnecessary deaths both in Iraq and Afghanistan but they could not have been avoided. I will tell you why. When we go to war no matter where it is our troops always wear some type of uniform. This enables them to stand out and be able to tell who is who. This is not the case for either the Taliban or al-Qaeda. The both of them do not wear any type of uniform and they have young children help fight the war. They send women, children, young and old as suicide bombers to kill unnecessary. I hate to say this but we have to put a stop to this insane type of combat. I tell the troops that if they suspect anyone being a suicide bomber no matter how old they are shoot first ask questions later. Also if they are in combat and someone is suspected of having any type of weapon to use against us then they also need to be killed. I have to say we must kill them and not give these people any more chances to kill us. If we do it this way then I say the war will be over within five years or sooner. I know some of you may not think President Obama is doing the right thing going to war again in Iraq. I myself thought the same thing. The other day I was talking to a friend of mine about all of this. We both agreed that President Obama is doing the right thing. If we let the Taliban or al-Qaeda continue like they are then our security either abroad or at home are in danger. They are growing at a fast rate. We have the advantage right now with all of the technology there is today to wipe them out a lot sooner than 5 years. We have the

drones to send out that are not manned. If we use these
more a lot of our own soldier's lives would be saved.
Not only would a lot of lives be saved but also a
lot of the wounded would be cut down in half. This is
the best way we should fight. We need not to waste any
more time or lives with the Taliban or al-Qaeda. Let us
stop them now, shoot to kill. I do not like to fight this
way however we are given no choice.

We need to go into whatever country we suspect the
enemy to be in. Even if it is in Pakistan, if they are there
then yes we will be there also. I do not care about any
type of agreement or treaty with any county. If they are
our allies then we will have no need to attack their
country. The only reason we will attack is if we suspect

either the Taliban or al-Qaeda solders to be there. Then we will use whatever force we need to wipe them out. Sad to say again innocent people are going to get killed. I also have to tell all of those innocent people that do not what to die they need to get out of their country. Go immediately to the United States Embassy of their country and they will be helped. When someone comes to us for help they have to surrender all of their possessions. They will be given new clean cloths similar to what they are wearing when they come to our Embassy. This is for security purposes. They will not be allowed to bring anything with them; all possessions they bring will be confiscated and cannot be returned.

This will make it easy for those who are asking for our help. The only ones we are after are the ones that like to fight dirty. I have to tell those who may be reading this we are going to fight dirty also. If we the United States of America follow this plan then all of the Taliban or al-Qaeda will all be killed before the five years is up. This also goes for whatever is going on in our own country.

We also need to ask any companies that are making any and all types of contracts to help win the war to lower their prices. This will help the United States to win the war. Also what ever happened to US savings bonds? If we the people of today would go back to buying US Savings bonds then this will not only help us win the war but also help the United States to get back on our feet. Yes I realize our country is heading to financial bankruptcy. The dollar in the entire world is losing its value. If we would help our own country first then we can help others. Not too long ago Secretary of State John Kerry secretly sent $1.3 billion in U.S. military aid to Muslim Brotherhood-controlled Egypt, waiving the restrictions put in place by Congress to withhold such aid unless the country could meet certain democracy standards. I obtained this information on the website below 1. I have to say how in the hell can we do this when we do not have any money for our own country. Yes there are a lot of countries that are in need of help. A lot of our third world countries are having it real bad. They are in need of good medical care, food, clothing and more. It is not up to our government to help these countries but it is up to us. We as a country cannot afford to donate money to any countries overseas. However churches can and are raising money to help these counties out. This is the only way we the United States of America can help anyone out. Our own government must get back on our feet. Until we do then we cannot send any money at all overseas.

Foot Notes

1. ww.theblaze.com/stories/2013/06/07/john-kerry-quietly-waives-law-put-in-place-by-congress-sends-muslim-brotherhood-controlled-egypt-1-3-billion-gift/

Chapter Three

President Obama

I have to tell you the truth lately I have been against

President Obama. However, there are a lot of things he is

doing that I do like and just a few I do not like. First of

all I am so happy that we finally got our first black

President. I can remember when he ran for his first term

in office. On election night NBC news project Obama

as being our 44th President. The news showed Jesse

Jackson with tears in his eyes at that same time I also

had tears in my own eyes.

Once he got into office he did not waste any time. Our roads started to get worked on. Still to this day a lot of highways are still getting work done on them. This is an unending job. There are so many roads today that are badly in need of work it is just too hard to get them done right away.

He has been doing things a President should not be doing at all. However if congress would get back to work and stop taking a vacation every week then he would not have to do their work. Yes a lot of things President Obama is doing are illegal but again I say if congress would do their work then he would not have to do it himself.

The only thing right now I can think of he is doing wrong is Obama Health Care. How in the hell can business and our people afford health care under Obama Care? There are a lot of things that can save Medicare and Medicaid a lot of money. If our own country would adopt a similar system that Canada has we would be a lot better off. The only thing I do not like about Canada's system is it takes way too long for any type of care or surgery to get approved.

President Obama needs to re work his health care before he leaves office. As you read more into this book you will see many different ways that would help out our health care system. We need to make a lot of changes. Some of the changes will cost money in the beginning but in the long run the changes will not only save our country money but also will save a lot of lives. In order for our government to get out of debt we need to make a lot of changes. It can be done but it is up to us to make the changes. The government has way too much to say and we the people are letting them get away with it.

Chapter Four

The Health Care System

As we all know our health care system is a mess. If we continue on the tract it is going then our country and ourselves will be bankrupt. The Obama Health Care Act needs to be looked at very carefully. If I am right congress did not even take a look at the proposal President Obama gave them. Speaker Nancy Pelosi gave some 2200 pages of the Obama Health Care Act and told congress just to sign it. There is a lot to what President Obama wants to have done in his health care act. What I like is the health care system Canada has. The only thing I object to in their system is when it comes to either elective surgery or surgery in general it takes way too long to have it approved. President Obama does want to make changes but congress is not helping nor are they letting him.

The other thing about our health care in general is costing us way too much money. For example if a person has cancer the treatments alone are very costly. If they do not have the proper insurance this can hurt not only them but it can be very devastating to the family. You figure if a person's bill is $100,000.00 and they have to pay 20% then their out of the pocket expense is

$20,000.00. The average American cannot afford this at all. The hospitals, doctors, and whoever else provides health care to us needs to take a better look at their charges. We have seen way too much stress on the family member who also suffers. Sometime families can lose their homes due to the high cost we are being charged. I tell you how I have always felt the 20% we are left over to pay we should not have to pay it at all. I do not myself, I let it go to collections and this forces our hospitals, doctors and health care providers to do their part in helping lowering the cost of health care in America. Some people are lucky and they have another insurance to pay that 20%. Just look at the charges it cost to have a MRI done and all of the people that pay the normal charge. I am not certain however I am sure the MRI is paid for within a year. If we continue to pay the high price of any and all tests or procedures then we will be forced into bankruptcy. If you think about it if a person files bankruptcy on any medical bill then the provider will not get paid at all. At least if a person pays the 80% their insurance pays the provider and they will get their money. Also for those people that are fortunate to have a secondary insurance the provider will then get the

100% of the charges.   This will not only help the patient

and but it will also help the providers.

    If we all follow my suggestions then not only the

patient but it will also keep the providers from

bankruptcy. We will all be happy I am sure.

Chapter Five

Our Mental Health System

All most every day now we hear on the news

shootings in our schools, churches, court rooms, streets

and way too much more. Why is this happening? I tell

you why. There are way too much budget cuts for

mental illness. Several years ago in my own county,

Warren County, NJ one of our only psychiatric hospital

was closed for good. Now Jan 1, 2015 we are once

again going to loose the only psychiatric behavior wards

in our hospital in Phillipsburg, N.J... Now if this

continues where are those with severe mental illness going to go? The only answer I would have to say is they will just go to the streets. Why would our own government let this happen? The decision starts right at our local government our councilman/woman, mayor, congressman/woman, governor, senator and last but least our president. Our government really needs to look better on how they manage our money. What we need as a Country is get control on our government. If we let congress do nothing like they are doing right now then sad to say but our country will just continue on the course it is on right now. We as a people can make this change by writing our councilman/woman, mayor, congressman/woman, senator and even our president. If you do not know how to contact them send me your letters and I will make sure they go to the right people. Trust me we can make changes but it is up to us to start. Do not say to yourself well I am only one person how can I make things change? If you do not like the way our government is handling our affairs then speak up for yourself. Just like John F. Kennedy once said, "My fellow Americans, ask not what your country can do for you, ask what you can do for your country." I will go one step further with this, "Ask not what God can do for you, but what can you can do for God." We can make things change but once again my friends it is all up to us.

Email me or send me what you think. I will get back to you as soon as I can. Please let me know what town, county and state you live in so I can make sure your opinion is given to the right people.

God Bless each and every one of you and God Bless the USA!

Email address: bds07882@gmail.com

Chapter Six

Recycling is a must

What is happening to America the Beautiful? Where
is all of our garbage going to? People do not realize how
important it is to recycle anything and everything they
can. A lot of our electronics such as vcr,old tv, toasters
and whatever else you have to plug into the wall are all
recyclable. I did not realize it until recently how much
metal and coper is in a lot of our electronics which are
going to our landfills on a daily basis. We as a people
can put a stop to it. How you may ask? Very simple

recycle, recycle, recycle. It is not hard. Just separate anything that can be recycled. Just about anything we use today can be recycled. All of our plastic containers are able to be recycled. Any paper and cardboard products can be recycled. Think before you put anything in your garbage can. If you are not sure it can be recycled then find out. I say this not only to the private sector but to any and all business including hospitals.

Our local government needs to crack down on people and businesses which do not recycled.

Once we all get use to a system which helps it will make it easier to recycle then it will not be hard at all.

The sooner the better we all start the less garbage

which will end-up in our landfills.

Start Today! RECYCLE AMERICA PLEASE!

NO FOOD – PLEASE EMPTY ITEMS

Chapter Seven

Lawsuits

As in regards to law suits I believe we as a people
have the right to sue. However on the other hand it is
way out of control. We see today on TV all the time
Lawyers are advertising about people who have taken
different medications and had bad reactions to them or
have even died. Medications can either help some
people or not. Every medication differs from person to
person. Today on each bottle or should be on each bottle
are adverse reactions a person may have. For example I

was put on one medication and I had a very bad reaction to it. I know someone who is on the same medication and he feels great on it.

Now today we also see on TV how people are either very sick or near death because of the addiction to nicotine. Why does our government not stick up for us when we go and sue the tobacco companies. If we are able to sue the tobacco companies then maybe they will stop putting many different chemicals that make us very addicted to them. Look at all of our teens today they are getting hooked on smoking it is not funny. I talked in another chapter about how we in America are going bankrupt because of the health care system. If we add up money wise how much it cost just one person who has gotten very sick from smoking it just makes me sick.

I myself a previous smoker have COPD. I was able to quit smoking by the grace of God. Yes I still today get sick because of my nasty habit I had years ago. I started smoking when I was 18 years old and instantly became addicted.

I feel sorry for all of our youth today that are smoking now. If they continue to smoke they will also get very sick from it. However; if they quit now it will add more and healthier years to each of their lives.

Let us not allow the tobacco companies to kill not

only the adults of today but also adults of tomorrow. We need to hit them where it will counts. Yes right where it is killing us, in our pocket books. We have the right to sue. Why then is our own government not helping us to help the health care system? I would like to know the answer.

Good luck to all of those who read this chapter and decided to quit smoking. I did it so can you.

Chapter Eight

Our Police Force

We need to thank each and every Police Officer whether they are male or female. They risk their lives every day. It does not matter anymore where they are working in, their lives are at risk. I can remember a few years ago one of our own police officers was sent on a call. It was about a car driving by and hitting mail boxes damaging them. Well it turned out to be a few youths thinking they were out having fun. Suddenly this fun they thought they were having almost ended an officers life. One of the persons in the car had a gun and started to shoot at the police car. One of the bullets almost killed the patrolman who was sent on the call. He luckily survived this call.

We hear today how police are shooting at people needlessly. Well if you would just listen to each case then I think you would do the same thing yourself. I heard on the news today of two cases. One a police officer shot at a person in a car who was wanted for armed robbery. This person shot and killed a person he was robbing. The police officer warned the person to put his hands on the dashboard of his car. When he was warned three times the person continued to make movements, the officer shot and killed him. Was the officer at fault, hell no he was just protecting us and also himself. Another incident recently was when a male in a car had a gun. When he was pulled over the police officer saw the gun and of course shot him. The gun turned out to be a bb gun but how was the officer able to tell at the time it was only a bb gun. This must stop. If anyone has a weapon then yes the police have the right to not only protect themselves but also protect us.

I like the idea the police officers will wear a camera attached to their uniform. Then we will see what actually is happening on each call. This is not only to protect the police but also to protect the innocent. I think in today's times and technology it warrants a devise like

this for every law enforcement officer. It does not

matter if they are local, state or federal officers.

Chapter Nine

Discrimination

Discrimination is a very touchy subject for all. We find all kinds of people being discriminated against no matter what sex, sexual preference, color, nationality, age and more. We as Americans must stop using the word discriminate as a reason or excuse for what is done to them. Yes I have to admit people are being decimated against still. It is not only the black people that are being discriminated against by Spanish, Muslims, White, Gay, Straight and more. Let us look at the OJ Simson trail back in 1995. If he was not acquitted like he was there would have been a riot throughout most of the United States. I can remember, at the time I lived in Florida. At the factory I worked at were some black people. They were saying that if OJ was found guilty there would be rioting in our own area. I can image what it was like in California where the trail was being held. Now this was a pure example because the color of a person a guilty man was set free. Thank God later on in years he was guilty on other charges having nothing to do with the case back in 1995. Today too many times the word discrimination comes to all nationalities. We can take a good look when our ancestors came over seas. They had to learn the langue of the country they came to. We need to speak the English language not matter where they come from if they are in public. I remember when I was in high school there was a class called, "English as a Second Language." This is totally wrong. English needs to be the first language. I think it is very rude someone that is in line buying something speaking another language. Our ancestors' years back learned the English language and spoke it in public. I do not care what language people use at home that is their business but what is said in public is Our Business. We need to bring the English langue back to America. I hate to say but if we do not get control on this then what language will be spoken in ten years to come? It will be Spanish. I am not discriminating at all with not only the black people but also the Spanish. I have had friends over the years that are both either black or Spanish. When I was in high school I took two years of Spanish. When I was at my friend's house I would speak Spanish to their parents. They both were taking English classes. By me doing this I was able to speak Spanish also his parents was learning English.

We all need to think a second time before we say that we are being discriminated against. Martin Luther King Jr. died trying to overcome discrimination against the black people. He did this peacefully yet he was still sent to jail. This in my opinion was not right. We all have a right to speak our mind but we need to do it peacefully. We have all come a long way since he was gunned down in 1968. We all need to continue his dream. I remember the famous words he had said, "Free at Last Free at Last Thank God Almighty I am Free at last." This came from an old song

"FREE AT LAST"

From "American Negro Songs " by J. W. Work.

Free at last, free at last
I thank God I'm free at last

Free at last, free at last
I thank God I'm free at last

Way down yonder in the graveyard walk
I thank God I'm free at last
Me and my Jesus going to meet and talk
I thank God I'm free at last

On my knees when the light pass'd by
I thank God I'm free at last
Tho't my soul would rise and fly
I thank God I'm free at last

Some of these mornings, bright and fair
I thank God I'm free at last
Goin' meet King Jesus in the air
I thank God I'm free at last

Chapter Ten

Volunteering

There are a lot of different ways a person can become

a volunteer. America is desperately in need of

volunteers in today's world. There are people that are

either on Social Security Disability or Supplement

Security Income whom are able to work. Even if it is

just a few hours a week at least they are putting back into

society. I do realize there are some people that are

collecting SSD who cannot work at all. However there

are a lot of people collecting SSI or SSD that can work

but do not want to. Is this right? No there are jobs out there even if it is waiting tables, working at McDonalds, being a cashier at any convenience store. It all is a honest living. We need to stop asking the government for handouts. I myself presently am on SSD due to my mental illness. There is a time very soon when I will thank the American People for helping and supporting me when I was in need. All the time I was on SSD I always worked a part time job. Just last year 2013 I was not working at all so I became a volunteer first aider for Phillipsburg Emergency Squad in Phillipsburg, NJ. I was a first aider years ago back in the 80's for Budd Lake First Aid Squad which was in Mt. Olive NJ. I enjoyed being a volunteer. Yes being on the first aid squad no matter where you are there will be those hard calls. I remember when I was on the Budd lake Squad I assisted delivery three babies. Now that was the happy calls I had. It did not matter how bad the call was I knew I was helping someone. Yes we had our calls where the person died but we were there to help console the family. There are a lot of other volunteer jobs that are just as important. I remember years ago when the hospitals had volunteers, they were called at that time, "Candy Stripers." They would assist the nurses back then. I would like to see a type of program come back to the hospitals. We often see hospitals are short staff because of extreme budget cuts. This is not fair at all to either the workers or patients. I was in the hospital recently. One night I remember when I asked for pain medicine it took at least 1 ½ hours. The nurse at that time was tending to another patient where if they had more help this would not happen. It is not the workers fault at all. They just need more help. If we bring more people in to volunteer whether it is a nurses aid, first aiders, fire fighters or whatever else this will help America. It will not only help our country but it will help the individuals whom are collecting either SSD or SSI. Like myself I never thought I would be able to give up my Social Security Income but thanks to me persevering I will be able to.

Not all people who are on either SSD or SSI will be able to do this I understand. It is the effort they make which counts. If you are able to and have the time become a volunteer. Help America and Help yourself.

Chapter Eleven

Violence in America

We are seeing it way too many times a person has

been shot and killed. Years ago on the news we would

hardly see, Special Bulletin" Now today we are seeing

this on our TV almost every day.

I have been in the Court Room in Paterson NJ last

year. This one case they were holding at the time

involved 3 youths and one youth whom had been killed.

The three youths belonged to a gang and this was

nothing new to them. Each of them was able to say

something to the mother who just lost her son because of them. They all were in remorse of what they had done. There are many big cities just like Paterson where there are gangs and they do not care who they shoot. The case I just spoke about was three black youths and the youth they murdered also was black. Now when this happens the other way around where a white person shoots and kills a black man all of the protests start up. Al Sharpton right away uses the Race Card. My question is why do we not hear Al Sharpton when a black youth kills another back youth. What we need for both Al Sharpton and Jesse Jackson is come to the cities like Patterson, Camden, Newark and more across the USA. I would like to see them speak and work with the youth. It would be ideal if the gangs would find something constructed to do with their time. There are also a lot of drugs in these big cities. I think if both Jesse Jackson and Al Sharpton took action then we can see some peace happening in our cites

Chapter Twelve

Global Independence

Our country has always helped other countries out whether it would be financially or spiritually. America as a country can no longer support any countries financially. We ourselves are on the verge of bankruptcy. I have always believed in helping our 3rd world countries. A lot of them are in need of food, medical supplies and more. If we as a people and not a country help out these 3rd world countries out then let us do it together. A lot of our churches are able to help these countries out. They are in need of our help I have to admit and this is a great way to do it. We not only send them money but we also send clothing, medical supplies these are just some ways we help the countries out.

Once our country is back on our feet then yes we should help other countries out. If these countries do not get help soon then there will be so many needless deaths in each of their country. If you yourself are able to help these countries out contact your church. If you do not attend church then contact any of your local churches. They will be able to tell you how you can help these unfortunate countries out.

I pray for all of these 3rd world countries in our world today. You also can help each of them by your individual prayer.

Chapter Thirteen

Our Government

Each person in our government is very important. It does not matter if they are our councilman/woman, mayor, congressman/woman, senator or even the president they all play a very important role in our government. It does not matter if it is our local government or federal these people are very important. If you do not like anything in your town then start contacting your councilman/woman. If you do not get any help then go as high as you need to do. Eventually your voice will be heard. They key part is you. It does not matter if we disagree the important thing is agree to disagree. We as an individual can and will make a difference. We all need to speak our opinion not matter what our belief is.

Congress in my opinion needs to work more with the president. Our current president Barack Obama has a lot of good ideas but congress just will not give him a chance. I would like to see our congress whether they are democrat or republican work together. This would make our country a lot stronger. When we see our government not working with each other the country is totally out of control. We not only see it now but we have seen it as far back as Abraham Lincoln. When

President Lincoln wanted to free the slaves both sides of congress was feuding over this. I realize both sides may not agree on certain bills, laws or what the public would like to see but just agree to disagree. This would help our government tremendously.

Closing Thoughts

The thirteen items on my agenda is just the beginning of what we as a nation needs to do. There is so much that needs to be done and I admit it will not happen overnight. If we stick together and push our government into doing the things which we believe needs to be address then we can accomplish them all a lot faster. It is up to our government to make things happen. Sad to say if congress continues on the course they are going right now then we will be in a lot worse shape than we are in right now.

As I mentioned in the beginning of this book if you have any comments and would like your voice to be heard then by all means contact me. We must unite as a country and I pray that we will.

God Bless each and every one of you and God Bless our United States.

Email me at bds07882@gmail.com

Bruce Dolan Smith

Credits

Pictures Courtesy from the following:

princessmoss.com

www.twu.edu

https://images.search.yahoo.com/images